IMAGES
of America

LAMBERTVILLE
AND
NEW HOPE

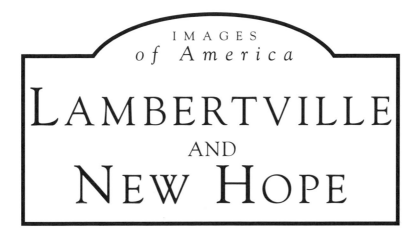

IMAGES
of America

LAMBERTVILLE
AND
NEW HOPE

James Mastrich, Yvonne Warren,
and George Kline

ARCADIA

First published 1996
Copyright © James Mastrich, Yvonne Warren, and George Kline, 1996

ISBN 0-7524-0285-4

Published by Arcadia Publishing,
an imprint of the Chalford Publishing Corporation
One Washington Center, Dover, New Hampshire 03820
Printed in Great Britain

Library of Congress Cataloging-in-Publication Data applied for

This book is dedicated
to all who lived, worked, and laughed at Coryell's Crossing
and to Zachary and all young people.
By learning about the past,
they may better love their home here on the Delaware River.

Contents

Acknowledgments

Giving birth to this book has been a genuine pleasure. There is no doubt in our minds that, were it not for the valued assistance and interest of a number of individuals, the book would not have become what we believe to be an accurate representation of life in Lambertville and New Hope in a time gone by.

Among the following, some offered their own precious photographs and some were very generous with historical information in their area of expertise. We are forever grateful and thank: Edward J. Carmody; Joseph Cavallaro; Faith Crown; Francis M. Curley; Pastor Joseph DiPaolo; Robert Gerenser; John C. Hazen; Janet Marsh Hunt; the Lambertville Historical Society; Warren F. Lee and Catherine T. Lee, authors of *Down Along the Old Bel-Del*; Fred Lewis; Jeffrey McVey; James L. Magill; Thomas Markey; the New Hope Historical Society; Jack Rosen; Betsy Smith, librarian, for her eager cooperation; and the Spruance Library at the Bucks County Historical Society, for access to their extensive collection of J.A. Anderson photographs. We also wish to thank Kathryn Hall for her editorial comments on an earlier draft.

One

Industry and Commerce

Ice cutting was a seasonal industry in New Hope until the weather began to moderate and the Delaware River stopped freezing over. In this photograph John McCauley, steward at the nearby Logan Inn, is supervising the operation. (Photograph courtesy of James Magill.)

The Delaware River has long defined the character of the Lambertville-New Hope area. Its very presence is responsible for one of the oldest industries in the region: commercial fishing, which has long been a main contributor to the economies of Lambertville and New Hope, as well as many other communities along the river's edge. Although the Delaware River has been known for its striped bass, trout, carp, catfish, walleyed pike, and sturgeon, it is the river's shad that claim the greatest renown. Immortalized by Ella Fitzgerald in the song "Lets Fall in Love," the shad have been commercially fished along the Delaware for well over one hundred years. In the 1950s, the late William Lewis wondered why the shad that he had harvested in abundance since the 1880s had virtually disappeared. In fact, in 1953 and again in 1956, no shad at all were seined. It was eventually learned that pollution from the industrial sites around Philadelphia and Trenton was responsible. Oxygen-depleted sections of the river called "pollution blocks" had formed as a result of raw sewage entering the river, and these eventually stopped the shad from migrating upstream to spawn. Today there is only one commercially-licensed fishery on the river. Traditions are held dear on the Delaware, however: the fishery is run by William Lewis's son Fred.

Another early commercial activity was the milling of feed and grain. An obvious advantage to locating near the basin of the Delaware River is the use of water as a means of power. The Parry Mill, operated in the 1700s, is a good example of early industry on the Delaware. Mr. Parry's mill utilized the water from Ingham Spring Creek that naturally flowed down to the Delaware by "borrowing" it just before the water reached its final destination. As a result he was able to establish a profitable business, provide for his family, and benefit the town. The Bucks County Playhouse is now located in the old Parry Mill building.

Numerous other business ventures took advantage of the plentiful water resources in this area. Several silk mills operated along the streams in the New Hope area and employed a great many people. Across the Delaware, the Lear Mill and the Prallsville Mill were among the grain and saw mill operations that stimulated the local economy. Over time, industry in the area became increasingly complex and diverse.

During the latter half of the nineteenth century and into the early twentieth, the Lambertville-New Hope area was a beehive of commercial and industrial activity. While both towns boasted numerous paper manufacturing operations, Lambertville was also "blessed" with huge factories producing rubber products. One of these facilities, the New Jersey Rubber Company, was known by local residents as the "Stink Mill." While there is no doubt that these paper and rubber factories resulted in a deterioration in the area's air quality, they were also responsible for a tremendous economic lift in both communities.

The development of manufacturing prompted the development of a transportation infrastructure, and this infrastructure in turn stimulated industry. The canals were built in the 1830s, and the railroad followed in the 1850s. The continued operation of the canals and railroads not only fostered the growth of other businesses, but also became industries in their own right, employing thousands of workers. For instance, many locomotive engines were produced by local workers in the machine shops of the Belvidere Delaware Railroad.

The images in this book are testimony to the idea that the only thing that is constant is change. Many business and industrial concerns in the area have been transformed over time, if not replaced entirely by more "modern" businesses. The "Mom and Pop" stores that were prevalent at the turn of the century gave way to the Acme Market and the Atlantic and Pacific Tea Company, with their popular and innovative packaged foods. Something is always lost in such transitions, but hopefully enough is gained to prevent too much longing for the "way things used to be."

The Lambertville and New Hope area tends to benefit from such developments. For example, the India Rubber Company, along the canal on Route 29, began producing rubber products in 1860. The original building has now been renovated to fit the needs of the retail businesses currently housed there. Directly across the river on Route 32, the Union Paper Manufacturing Company has been transformed into a bank of luxury townhouses overlooking the river. The two train stations have been adapted to uses that are particularly appreciated by the locals: the Lambertville Depot is now a thriving restaurant, and the old Reading Terminal in New Hope is successful in transporting tourists.

Because the Lambertville and New Hope area has been a transportation hub from the days of horses and carriages through to the days of the automobile, it has also been an ideal location for industry to both thrive and evolve. Through the photographs in this chapter we follow the progression from an agrarian and commercial economy through the Industrial Revolution and on to the diversification that took place in the early twentieth century. Over time, the nature of the communities has changed as different industries have come and gone but all of the commercial activities and changes contributed to laying the foundation for what is now a very pleasant place to visit or live.

Cut ice was loaded onto a wagon and taken to the Logan Inn to be used in the kitchen and bar. In 1909 New Hope native John W. Kooker began making artificial ice. His and other ice-manufacturing ventures would eventually eliminate the natural ice business. (Photograph courtesy of James Magill.)

The Lewis shad crew is shown here tending the nets. Living along the Delaware meant fishing for shad and history books tell us that it has always been this way. The Lenni Lenape Native Americans actually taught the European settlers to use the nets that are still employed today. In 1851 the going price for one hundred shad in the Philadelphia markets was $17. (Photograph courtesy of George Kline.)

Boy Willie Smith was photographed mending the shad nets. The nets are called seines and the fishermen seine for the shad by setting the seines in the flow of the river. The seines are hung vertically in the water to catch the fish and are then pulled hand-over-hand to the shore. Even today shad crews are often comprised of members of families that have traditionally been very involved with shad fishing. (Photograph courtesy of George Kline.)

John Holcombe carried on the Lenni Lenape tradition of fishing from Holcombe Island around 1777. In 1888 the Lewis family bought The Point Fishery that was located on this site and hired Boy Willie Smith to manage the operation. At that same time William Lewis also coordinated the operation of the Ferry Fishery in New Hope. (Photograph courtesy of Lambertville Historical Society.)

The Child Store, the Pearline General Store, and Buse's Grocery delivery wagon served many of the needs of the residents of New Hope in the 1850s. Records from the Trenton market show that at this time butter cost 25¢ per pound, corn cost 8¢ per dozen, and blackberries cost 6¢ per quart. The street leading down to the water is Ferry Street. Ferry Street in New Hope mirrors its sister street in Lambertville as the arrival and departure point for the ferry trip across the Delaware. (Photograph courtesy of the Spruance Library at the Bucks County Historical Society.)

The C.V. Rittenhouse store was a popular mercantile company that did business at this site for many years. The upstairs section was used for social and political meetings, and here local businessmen would address matters similar to those discussed by modern-day chambers of commerce. The Rittenhouse store housed a pharmacy for a while, and is still used as a retail establishment. (Photograph courtesy of Mary Rittenhouse Smith.)

The bakery provided a necessary service in an age when many homes did not have adequate baking capabilities in their coal and wood stoves. Although man cannot live by bread alone, the bakeries certainly made life more pleasant. Note the old weight balance scale in this image. (Photograph courtesy of Lambertville Historical Society.)

The Atlantic and Pacific Tea Company brought many new grocery products to the residents of Lambertville and New Hope, as it was among the first stores to introduce prepackaged products. Note the familiar products that have stayed with us over time: Kelloggs, Heinz, Aunt Jemima, and Quaker Puffed Wheat! (Photograph courtesy of Lambertville Historical Society.)

At the turn of the century Lambertville residents could find all the groceries they needed at the stores grouped at the corner of Bridge and Union Streets. This photograph shows the awnings that the A&P Food Market used to protect its fresh produce from the hot summer sun. In 1893, electric lights first began to be used in businesses. (Photograph courtesy of George Kline.)

Lambertville folk are shown here going about their business on Bridge Street in 1907. At this time the street was still unpaved, and yet Shamalia's Drug Store possessed modern technology in the form of the first telegraph machine in town. If this photograph had been taken just four years before, in 1903, the old covered bridge would obscure the view across to New Hope. The covered bridge was lost in 1903. (Photograph courtesy of George Kline.)

The Lambertville House served as an inn from 1814 and has housed various business on its premises over the years. In this photograph of the second expansion of the inn, we can see Kerr & Green Clothing, Gents Furnishings, Hats and Fine Footwear. Note the silent policeman cautioning early drivers to "go slow and stay to the right"; a philosophy to which many politicians adhere. (Photograph courtesy of Lambertville Historical Society.)

The Conover and Conover Company was a full-service mercantile store complete with men's straw hats. Note the corrugated tin roof protecting the merchandise displayed on the sidewalk. These roofs were later replaced by roll-up awnings. The entire concept of locally-based businesses, unfortunately, was replaced when America began embracing malls. (Photograph courtesy of Lambertville Historical Society.)

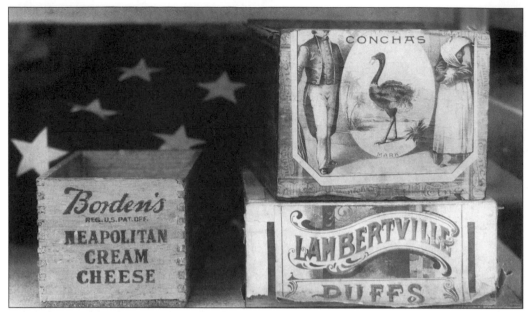

This photograph shows some of the many products sold at J.B. Kline's Segar Store in Lambertville. The "Puff" was a specialty cigar created and blended locally by J.B. Kline. Its name was derived from Kline's curious method of market research. He would stride up to one of Lambertville's lovely maidens, and, with her permission, puff a whiff of cigar smoke from one of his latest blends in her direction. Kline knew he had a winner if he received a pleasant sigh of approval. (Photograph courtesy of Jack Rosen.)

An advertisement for Frank Z. Fritz' Photo-Miniature and Photograph Gallery at 46 1/2 Coryell Street in Lambertville. At the time this advertisement was made Fritz specialized in ferrotypes. Ferrotypes—which are also known as tintypes—are positive photographs made directly on iron plates that are varnished with a thin, sensitized film. (Photograph courtesy of Joseph Cavallaro.)

In the early days business and commerce were transacted using the basic method of barter, and later by using federal greenbacks and scrip. This is a sheet of unused scrip issued by The New Hope Delaware Bridge Company. Under its first charter, the company had banking privileges and kept its vaults in the Delaware House in New Hope. Note the very fine detail of the figure drawings. (Photograph courtesy of James Mastrich and Kathryn Hall.)

On the columned entryway of the Hunterdon National Bank in Lambertville sits this cast bee hive. The busy bees were intended to symbolize the diligent efforts the bank assured its customers that it would employ to look after their money. The building is still used as a bank. (Photograph courtesy of James Mastrich and Kathryn Hall.)

In 1879, Milton B. Kline sold the retail department of his tobacco and cigar store to his brother, J.B. Kline, who is shown here with the "segar" store Indian he imported from Germany. He contracted with master woodcarvers in the Black Forest to create a beautiful "objet d'art" that would stand outside the J.B. Kline & Son Smoke Shop and attract customers. The Indian is gone, but a fanciful descendant of J.B. still attracts customers by telling colorful stories while playing the part of famous world leaders such as Churchill, Patton, or Kissinger. (Photograph courtesy of George Kline.)

This advertisement was painted on the side of the Enterprise Segar Store run by J.B. Kline & Son in Lambertville. In one year alone, over 250,000 cigars were sold and went up in smoke. This family business evolved into an elaborate postcard and greeting card shop, and even began offering office supplies and vintage musical instruments. It has many loyal customers and continues to be a thriving business today. (Photograph courtesy of George Kline.)

This photograph captures the scene at Union and Bridge Streets in Lambertville and also shows the Fisher Building, one of the homes of *The Beacon*. The partially-obscured sign on the far right, "Plain & Fancy," refers to the special printing services that the newspaper offered as a sideline to newspaper publishing. Although curbs had been installed by this time, the ladies of the town still continued to complain about the muddy streets. (Photograph courtesy of George Kline.)

The Beacon has reported the news for the Lambertville and New Hope area from 1885 to the present day. Phineas Kennedy Hazen came to Lambertville following his service in the Civil War, and acquired a newspaper service that had operated for forty years prior to his founding of *The Beacon*. In this era, several businesses would frequently share a building: in this case, *The Beacon* used the first floor while the Metropolitan Life Insurance business used the second floor. (Photograph courtesy of *The Beacon*.)

In *Paradise*, John Prine wrote: "Then the coal company came with the world's largest shovel; And they tortured the timber and stripped all the land; Well, they dug for their coal till the land was forsaken; Then they wrote it all down to the progress of man." This photograph shows the Goat Hill Quarry in 1905. (Photograph courtesy of Lambertville Historical Society.)

This is the George C. Green Garage and Machine Shop in Lambertville. As a boy of fourteen, Mr. Green began to work as his father's bookkeeper, but he discovered an innate talent for mechanics and soon began a lifelong career as a self-taught inventor. His talents and production techniques had a profound influence on the development of tool and die manufacturing. It was said that he could just look at a machine that was not operating properly and, without touching it, could tell you what was wrong. Green's garage is still used as a commercial building. (Photograph courtesy of Thomas J. Hood.)

This photograph shows the Lear Mill and the Fred Lewis Fishery building on Holcombe Island. The Lear Mill has seen use as a flour and feed mill and also as a saw mill. It burned in 1946. The tower of the Centenary Methodist Church can also be seen in the background peering over the treetops. (Photograph courtesy of George Kline.)

The Union Mills Paper Manufacturing Company was one of New Hope's biggest employers. It produced the extra-fine tissue paper used to wrap copper wire. One of their major customers was the John A. Roebling and Sons Company which was located 15 miles downriver in Trenton. In 1931, Ferdinand Roebling White became vice-president of the Union Mills and of the Universal Paper Bag Company, also located in New Hope. Apparently it was "all in the family." (Photograph courtesy of Lambertville Historical Society.)

This is the location of the Lambertville Spoke Manufacturing Company, the famous manufacturer of spokes, hubs, rims, poles, neck yokes, whiffle trees, and handles. Civil War historians note that a great many of the Union Army's wagon wheels and axles came from this company. Notice the supply of logs waiting to be used for production. (Photograph courtesy of George Kline.)

These are the waterwheels that produced the power to fuel the Union Mills Paper Manufacturing Company. A unique system of waterwheels was also employed to raise the water level in the nearby Delaware Canal by literally "wheeling" water from the Delaware River. (Photograph courtesy of George Kline.)

In 1909 the Lambertville Pottery—the second pottery in town—was completed and scheduled to begin manufacturing sanitary ware. By 1920, the company had six kilns in operation. In this scene we see the chimneys of the many kilns used in manufacturing. Lambertville Ceramics continues the tradition by producing continuous filament ceramic fibers through its unique Viscous Suspension Spinning Process. (Photograph courtesy of Yvonne Warren.)

The Industrial Revolution took full advantage of the talents of men and women, young and old alike. These men and women were some of the mill workers in Lambertville. (Photograph courtesy of Lambertville Historical Society.)

The New Jersey Rubber Company, formed in 1890, was lovingly referred to as the "Stink Mill" by local residents. It was known that for a time the exhaust and toxic debris from the manufacturing process killed the vegetation on Holcombe Island, the island located between the New Jersey Rubber Company and the Delaware River. (Photograph courtesy of Lambertville Historical Society.)

This photograph shows the Campbell Silk Hosiery Mills on Cherry Street in Lambertville. The beautiful building and the business it housed rose like a phoenix from the ashes of the infamous stock market crash of 1929. The company boomed until the development of nylons and other synthetics extinguished its flame during World War II. (Photograph courtesy of George Kline.)

The sprawling Lambertville Rubber Company can be seen in this view from Goat Hill. Industry expanded so greatly in Lambertville that its presence could be seen, and often smelled, on both sides of town and across the river into New Hope. Note the covered bridge in the background. (Photograph courtesy of George Kline.)

The Lambertville Rubber Company was particularly proud of certain items they manufactured: for instance, in 1876 the company shipped a rubber belt 318 feet long by 2 feet wide and weighing 1,600 pounds to a customer in New York. However, the company was most well known as the manufacturer of the Snag-Proof boots which it began producing in the same year. The boots became known across the country for their fine quality and it is said that the Lambertville Rubber Company went out of business because they never built obsolescence into their boots: there are still many pairs of Snag-Proof boots around today because they never wear out! (Photograph courtesy of James Mastrich and Kathryn Hall.)

Two
History

Since 1828, the metal Indian
has remained near the Logan
Inn as a "guardian" of New
Hope. The legend connected
with the Indian is that of a
Lenni Lenape chief noted for
the kindness and hospitality that
he offered the white settlers of
the area. He developed a close
relationship with James Logan,
secretary to William Penn, and
took his name. Chief Logan
ultimately withdrew his support
to the settlers, however, when
all of his relatives were killed in
a massacre in Ohio. (Photograph
courtesy of the Spruance Library
at the Bucks County Historical
Society.)

If the history of our two small communities in the Delaware Valley were written as a work of fiction, the story that develops could not unfold more perfectly than the actual chronicle of the events that took place here and the characters that took part in them. Few places in America have played as important a role in the shaping of this young country's destiny as Coryell's Ferry, a settlement that would become two communities—Lambertville and New Hope.

Coryell's Ferry was named after Emanuel Coryell, who began operating a ferry service across the Delaware in 1733. At that time it was common for such ferry services to be named after the man who operated them—Coryell's Ferry was known in earlier days as Well's Ferry, after another ferryman. The crossing was an important one, as it formed part of the main route from New Amsterdam (now New York) to Philadelphia.

This route, known as the York Road or the King's Highway since the actual construction of a road in 1769, was the main cause of early commercial development in Coryell's Ferry, as businesses such as the Logan Inn, the Delaware House, and the Lambertville House were established to cater to stagecoach traffic.

Originally the tracts of land on both sides of the Delaware were granted to William Penn by the King of England, but by various means they later fell into the hands of private owners, who were in a large part responsible for the direction that the towns of Lambertville and New Hope were to take. One development that ensured that the towns would remain and continue as "twin river hamlets" was the construction of the first bridge between the communities. On September 25, 1811, a group of men from New Hope and Lambertville met at the Logan Inn (then called the Ferry Tavern) to discuss plans to build a bridge joining the two communities and formed the New Hope Delaware Bridge Company. The covered bridge was first crossed in mid-January 1814, and it stood until 1841, when a portion of it was carried away during a freshet. Its replacement, also a covered bridge, stood until it was destroyed in the Great Flood of 1903.

Lambertville and New Hope have always had a great deal in common, but as they grew they developed in slightly different ways. New Hope was christened by a member of one of its most prominent families, the Parrys. Benjamin Parry, a very distinguished businessman, acquired the Prime Hope Mills in 1784 and in the same year built the beautiful Parry Mansion. The family and the town prospered, but six years later tragedy struck when the grist mill burned to the ground. Mr. Parry stated to a local newspaper at the time, "I am rebuilding with new hope," and the community was known as New Hope ever after. The name may be said to have been a good omen, as New Hope became the leading industrial town in Bucks County in the nineteenth century, with paper mills, an iron foundry, and several silk-manufacturing operations. These operations did not detract from the area's natural beauty, however, and by the early 1900s New Hope began attracting artists such as Edward W. Redfield, William L. Lathrop, and Daniel Garber, who formed part of what is known as the New Hope School of Painting.

On March 1, 1849, Lambertville was incorporated as a borough, with Samuel Lilly, M.D., serving as its first mayor. The first prominent citizens in the community were members of the Coryell and Holcombe families, but the town was ultimately named after a member of one of the relatively new families, the Lamberts. John Lambert was a senator during the Jefferson administration and in 1814 he procured the first post office for the town. The "honorable" senator then called the town "Lambert's Ville" and appointed his nephew as postmaster.

Just as New Hope developed during the Industrial Revolution, Lambertville grew even larger, with huge paper mills, rubber mills, iron foundries, and pottery works sprawling along the river. As Hunterdon County's only city, Lambertville was frequently included on the presidential campaign trail, and Grover Cleveland, William Taft, Theodore Roosevelt, Woodrow Wilson, Franklin Delano Roosevelt, Harry S. Truman, and Horace Greeley have all visited. Even the perennial Democratic candidate William Jennings Bryan spoke to an overflow crowd in Lambertville from the rear of his campaign train in September 1896 and again in October 1908.

Area residents had strong sentiments about the Civil War, yet readily supplied their share of men to raise the regiments sought throughout the countryside. Cassions needed by the Union Army were made by the Finney Spoke Manufacturing Company in Lambertville, making the company's owner a fortune at the same time. Civil War monuments and cannons in both towns proudly and solemnly commemorate the war experience.

Lambertville and New Hope seem to have produced and been home to a disproportionately large number of talented and famous people. Who knows? Perhaps there is something in the water. Many of these individuals started a ripple in their own areas of expertise that ultimately reached far and wide and this continues today. The images and accompanying captions that follow give us some insight into the background of such characters and the impact that they had. Hopefully, this will enable us to better understand the history of Lambertville and New Hope and also where they are heading in our times.

The Logan Inn was erected as a tavern in 1727 by John Wells, who ran the ferry at that time. It was originally called the Ferry Tavern, but it was renamed the Logan House about one hundred years after it was first licensed. The current name, the Logan Inn, was a later name change. The building itself has also been altered over the years: the most significant alteration was a typical Colonial enlargement, achieved by wrapping additions around the existing structure. (Photograph courtesy of George Kline.)

James Wilson Marshall was born in Marshall's Corner, New Jersey. During his childhood he lived on Bridge Street in Lambertville in the building that is now the headquarters of the Lambertville Historical Society. Marshall was an adventurous young man who took a daring chance when he joined a wagon train heading west on the Oregon Trail. He later became famous for discovering a nugget of gold at Sudder's Mill, California, in 1848, thus beginning the California Gold Rush of 1849. He was known to have been generous to many, but he died a poor man in Placerville, California, in 1885. (Photograph courtesy of Lambertville Historical Society.)

The James Wilson Marshall Museum is located in Marshall's childhood home. Marshall is an important figure in the history of the United States: his discovery touched off the infamous frenzied activity of the 49ers. In 1948 the United States Postal Service issued a 3¢ stamp titled "California Gold Centennial, Sutter's Mill, Coloma, California" to commemorate the centennial of the event. (Photograph courtesy of Lambertville Historical Society.)

The Thompson-Neely House is known as the "House of Decision." When General Washington surveyed the lay of the land from Goat Hill in Lambertville he concluded that the Delaware formed a natural line of defense from the Pennsylvania side. He then crossed over to New Hope and met with his lieutenants at the Thompson-Neely House to discuss the plan that would eventually lead to the Battle of Trenton on December 25, 1776. (Photograph courtesy of the Spruance Library at the Bucks County Historical Society.)

The British stood atop Washington's Rock on Goat Hill to gain a clear view of the Pennsylvania side. What they could not see from this vantage point, however, were the Durham boats that Captain Daniel Bray had hidden behind Little Malta Island. Area resident Cornelius Coryell was selected as a "confidential agent" to keep watch over the boats that would later be used in Washington's famous crossing of the Delaware. He was successful, as the spies of Lord Cornwallis were not able to substantiate the report that Washington was collecting boats at Coryell's Ferry. (Photograph courtesy of George Kline.)

The area that is now the intersection of Bridge and Union Streets in Lambertville was a wheat field and an apple orchard when Washington's troops bivouacked here before repositioning for the march to Trenton. The large, flat-bottomed boats hidden downriver awaiting the troops were called Durham boats because they were originally constructed to transport iron from the Durham furnaces downriver to Philadelphia. (Photograph courtesy of George Kline.)

Washington's bold strategy required an initial crossing of the Delaware to New Hope. It was at this point, parallel to Main Street, that his troops began the 7-mile march south to McKonkey's Ferry Crossing. Because Washington was concerned that his left flank might be vulnerable he ordered Captain William Washington and Lieutenant James Monroe (the future president) to cross back over to Lambertville and position themselves at the Princeton Pike to prevent any British intelligence or reinforcements from Princeton from reaching Trenton. (Photograph courtesy of George Kline.)

George Washington and 2,400 Continental Army soldiers crossed the ice-clogged Delaware River at the site of the McKonkey House at Washington Crossing. They surprised the Hessian troops barracked downriver in Trenton on Christmas night, 1776, and won the Battle of Trenton. Colonel Rall, the Hessian commander, was seriously wounded in the battle and surrendered his sword to Washington. During the battle a note that he had placed unread in his pocket when it was given to him amidst the Christmas revelry of the night before fell from his coat. It was from a Tory farmer warning him of Washington's plan to attack. (Photograph courtesy of George Kline.)

The Black Bass Hotel, located upriver in Lumberville, Pennsylvania, was built in 1745 as a fortified haven for river travelers. Because the proprietor of the inn was loyal to the British, he refused to allow General Washington to enter the premises. It is interesting to note that, to this day, the Black Bass Inn remains steeped in Tory regalia and considers itself to be located in an occupied country. (Photograph courtesy of the Black Bass Inn.)

N.C. Wyeth's mural depicts Washington's reception in Trenton on April 21, 1789. Washington was on his way to New York to assume the duties of president. Before they crossed the Delaware, Washington had this excerpt from Thomas Paine's famous pamphlet, *The Crisis*, read to every soldier: "These are the times that try men's souls. . . ." Wyeth's painting is on display at One West State Street in Trenton. (Photograph courtesy of Corestates New Jersey National Bank.)

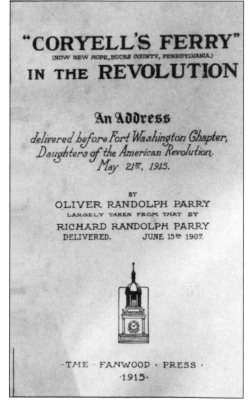

The Daughters of the American Revolution honored New Hope and Lambertville in 1915 by asking Oliver Randolph Parry to present this address. "Coryell's Ferry in the Revolution" was written by a member of a significant New Hope family, and it captures some of the pride that citizens of Lambertville and New Hope feel about their towns' place in American history. (Photograph courtesy of Joseph Cavallaro.)

This obelisk in the graveyard of the First Presbyterian Church in Lambertville marks the grave of General George Coryell, a member of General Washington's staff for a portion of the Revolutionary War. Coryell was the last survivor of the staff and he assisted as a pallbearer at Washington's burial in 1799. (Photograph courtesy of the Spruance Library at the Bucks County Historical Society.)

The York Road was for many years the main route for those traveling from New York to Philadelphia. The toll paid by each traveler or vehicle that passed through contributed to the cost of maintaining the road and tollbooths such as this one in New Hope. (Photograph courtesy of James Magill.)

In this photograph we see that the York Road's surface has improved greatly since the days when it was used primarily by stagecoaches and wagons. As the road crossed the private property of a variety of farmers and other landowners, it was very smooth and well-maintained in some places, while being full of ruts and potholes in others. (Photograph courtesy of James Magill.)

The cannon on South Main Street is a monument to the local men who did not return home from the Civil War. It sits at the base of a triangular piece of land in New Hope's historic district. The Dahlgren cannon was used aboard the USS *Minnesota* during the famous Civil War naval battle involving the *Monitor* and *Merrimack*. Unfortunately, the *Minnesota* was lost during the fray, but the cannon survived to serve as a reminder of the local men who died during the war. (Photograph courtesy of James Magill.)

This Civil War cannon sat on the west side of New Hope at the junction of Ferry Street and York Road, an area known as "Flat Iron Point." It was removed during road construction around 1950 and has been mysteriously missing since then. Technically called a "Parrot" rifle, it is particularly unique because it is one of the first breach-loading cannons ever produced. It was given to New Hope when the USS *Richmond* was decommissioned and transformed into a hospital ship. (Photograph courtesy of James Magill.)

This Civil War soldier was photographed by Tibbels, one of the many professional photographers in Lambertville. The soldier is representative of the volunteers in the regiments raised in Hunterdon and Bucks Counties to serve in the war. (Photograph courtesy of Joseph Cavallaro.)

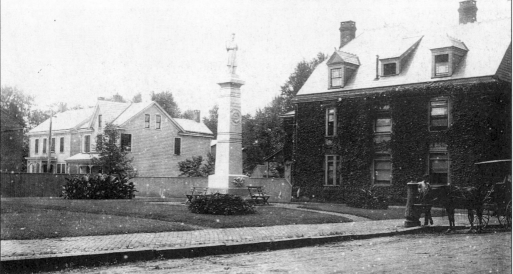

This monument was dedicated in 1870 to the memory of the soldiers of the Union Army who died during the Civil War. It is located in the Mary Sheridan Park in Lambertville. The cost of the war went beyond death and destruction: inflation during the war years was responsible for price increases of 300% for coal, 810% for cotton goods, and 343% for butter. The last item is clear evidence that when you opt for guns, you forgo the butter. (Photograph courtesy of Lambertville Historical Society.)

Ashbel Welch, one of America's most illustrious engineers, was a resident of Lambertville. Born in 1809, Welch was a humble and religious man. Among the many projects that he was involved with were the Delaware and Raritan Feeder Canal and the Belvidere Delaware Railroad. His ideas about creating an inter-oceanic canal greatly influenced the development of the Panama Canal project. (Photograph courtesy of Lambertville Historical Society.)

The Liberty Bell passed through Lambertville on its return to Philadelphia from the San Francisco Pan American Exposition on November 15, 1915. As the Liberty Bell Special approached Lambertville at 1:30 pm, it was greeted with a roar of factory whistles and the ringing of New Hope and Lambertville church bells. Schoolchildren sang patriotic songs and the local militia fired salutes into the air. The famous crack in the bell was caused by the pealing of the bell during the funeral of Chief Justice John Marshall in 1832. (Photograph courtesy of Martin Luther and Marcia Chapman.)

Three
The Canals

This photograph of New Hope and the Delaware Canal was taken by Roy Hutchinson from the top of the chimney at the Union Paper Mill in the late 1920s. Mr. Hutchinson, a machinist at the mill, took advantage of the mill's shutdown for maintenance to climb the metal ladder inside the great chimney and capture this image. (Photograph courtesy of James Magill.)

The canal passing through New Hope is known as the Delaware Canal. On the opposite side of the river, the Delaware and Raritan Feeder Canal runs through Lambertville. These canals and the Delaware River created a vital route for commerce in the industrial era and were partially responsible for the evolution of Lambertville and New Hope into such hubs of human activity.

Canal construction was grasped by nineteenth-century industrialists as a cost-effective method of transportation, but inland waterways had actually been thought of years before by leaders such as William Penn in the late seventeenth century and George Washington in the eighteenth century. Considering the problems inherent in organizing the movement of people and supplies across even small segments of their vast continent, both men seized upon the idea of inland waterways, but it was not until the beginning of the nineteenth century that conditions were right for the realization of their dreams.

The opening of the Erie Canal in 1825 caused an almost immediate explosion in the levels of commerce and immigration along its route. It then became clear to progressive legislators in both Pennsylvania and New Jersey that the economic future, if not the survival, of these states depended on the construction of an efficient network of canals. Their arguments must have been strong: by the late 1820s, the Pennsylvania Legislature allocated as much as three times the state's previous annual income for canal projects so that new canals, including the Delaware Canal, could be constructed and maintained. The New Jersey Legislature soon followed suit by chartering the Delaware and Raritan Feeder Canal project.

The Delaware Canal was intended as a support to the Lehigh Canal, which ran from the anthracite coal region down to Easton, Pennsylvania, at the point where the Lehigh River joins the Delaware River. The chief engineer for the project, Canvass White, is credited with the development of the hydraulic cement (a building material that hardens while immersed in water) that was particularly important in constructing the many locks in the Delaware Canal. While White's engineering talents provided for a sound design, Irish immigrants and local farmers physically dug out more than 60 miles of earth with picks, shovels, and wheelbarrows to create the canal. The first leg of the canal—from Bristol to New Hope—was operational by 1831, and in 1832, the second leg, the section that met the Lehigh Canal, was finished.

The main item carried on the canal was anthracite coal. Some of it would be unloaded in New Hope, where local residents would buy it in quantities of a ton or more from Phinas Slack and other local coal merchants. The coal was graded by a very simple system: each type corresponded to a common object of a similar size, hence "pea coal," "buckwheat coal," "chestnut coal," and "egg coal." The coal was delivered in horse-drawn wagons and shoveled by hand into customers' basements via coal chutes.

The canal boats also carried items such as lumber, limestone, cement, iron, produce, and even Bushkill whiskey on their outward trip. To make canal operations cost-effective, the canal boats also carried various items on their return trip, including manufactured goods, imported products, and even an occasional shipment of Jamaican rum.

The peak period of operations on the Delaware Canal was in the mid-nineteenth century. In 1855, for example, at least 755,000 tons of goods were transported. During that same year, 156,000 tons crossed the Delaware River at New Hope and entered the Delaware and Raritan Feeder Canal in Lambertville en route to Trenton or New York. In a system that was thought at the time to be a miracle of engineering, canal boats crossed the river from the open outlet lock of one canal to the open outlet lock of the other.

The Delaware and Raritan Feeder Canal was another innovative development that was vital in the overall operation of the canal network. In 1830, Canvass White appointed Ashbel Welch of Lambertville to his team of engineers. Welch became one of the foremost engineers of this period; his innovative theories on inter-oceanic canals were eventually used in the construction of the Panama Canal, and he also became president of the American Society of Civil Engineers and was made an honorary member of the Institute of Civil Engineers of Great Britain.

The construction of the Feeder Canal, like that of the Delaware Canal, was an extraordinary feat accomplished due to the intellectual and physical efforts of a talented team of engineers and laborers. The word "feeder" describes a vital function of the canal: not only did it transport goods to and from the market, but it also used water from the Delaware River to literally "feed" the series of canals that went further on to Princeton, Morristown, and Burlington, New Jersey. The Feeder is approximately 24 miles long, and it has only three locks: one each at Raven Rock and Prallsville, and an outlet lock at Lambertville. The total cost of construction of the Delaware and Raritan Feeder Canal was $1,500,000. The canal was officially opened on June 25, 1834, with a VIP excursion from Trenton to Lambertville that included dignitaries such as New Jersey Governor Peter D. Vroom.

This shot of canal mules feeding in New Hope is typical of a J.A. Anderson photograph. A local photographer, Anderson was known for his exemplary technique and for the excellent composition of his images. (Photograph courtesy of James Magill.)

These mule drivers took time from tending their mules in New Hope to pose for a photograph. The gentleman on the right is George Myers, who was affiliated with the Delaware Canal for many years. (Photograph courtesy of James Magill.)

This scene gives us a glimpse of the shear physical effort that went into canal construction. The work was exhausting, and sometimes the men in the company's employ did not believe their pay was commensurate with the effort expended. In 1852, those working on winter repairs on the Delaware and Raritan Feeder Canal rioted to publicize their demand for a pay rise. They were seeking a raise of 25¢, to take their daily wage from 75¢ to $1 per day. (Photograph courtesy of James Magill.)

Primitive cement machines such as this one were used in the construction of locks in New Hope. As late as 1894, well over nine hundred canal boats were towed across the Delaware River, usually from the Delaware Canal outlet lock in New Hope, to the Feeder Canal in Lambertville. (Photograph courtesy of James Magill.)

These men were photographed in 1910 while tending the canal boats at the outlet lock at the south end of New Hope. The boats are filled with goods for sale downriver, most likely in Trenton. Boats remaining in the Delaware Canal at this point were generally headed to Bristol. From there the cargo might be transferred to a river barge to make the trip to Philadelphia or points beyond. Note the hill in the background mirroring Lambert Hill and Goat Hill across the river. (Photograph courtesy of James Magill.)

This is the Delaware Canal tollhouse in New Hope. The fee paid depended upon the number of locks that would be crossed. A full fee in New Hope allowed for passage through all three locks, including the outlet lock to the Delaware and Raritan Feeder Canal in Lambertville. (Photograph courtesy of James Magill.)

This photograph was taken looking south from Mechanic Street in New Hope. As a canal boat approached a lock, the boatmen would blow through a conch shell to alert the lock-keeper to swing into action. (Photograph courtesy of Yvonne Warren.)

A canal boat is shown here leaving the outlet lock in Lambertville. Note the lock-keeper's house and the view of New Hope across the Delaware River. (Photograph courtesy of George Kline.)

Boat on Canal, New Hope, Penna.   5313

Reflected in the water of the Delaware Canal in New Hope is a canal boat, together with its teams of mules and mule drivers. Although there was a great deal of commerce and general business along both canals, lovely scenes such as this could be enjoyed just a few minutes outside of both New Hope and Lambertville. (Photograph courtesy of George Kline.)

This winter scene shows South Main Street and the Feeder Canal in Lambertville in 1939. The canal basin was where the canal boats were taken out of the water for maintenance. In 1832, during the construction of the Feeder, a disastrous epidemic of cholera broke out among the Irish canal workers living in a shanty town in this area south of Lambertville. Hundreds died before the disease ran its course. (Photograph courtesy of Yvonne Warren.)

In this J.A. Anderson photograph we can see much that tells the story of the twin river hamlets. The canal bridge in the foreground is part of Coryell Street in Lambertville. To the left of the bridge can be seen a group of covered canal boats in the Delaware and Raritan Feeder Canal. In the middle of the photograph is the covered bridge crossing over to New Hope. The hill in the background is Saint Martin's Hill. (Photograph courtesy of Lambertville Historical Society.)

In 1920, the Delaware and Raritan Feeder Canal still carried a great deal of merchandise, produce, and goods for sale downriver. In this scene we are able to see two connected canal boats as they pass some of the railroad buildings in Lambertville. (Photograph courtesy of Yvonne Warren.)

This pastoral scene of the Delaware and Raritan Feeder Canal was photographed looking north to Lambertville. There is clear evidence in this photograph that even long ago, people sometimes aired their dirty laundry. (Photograph courtesy of the Spruance Library at the Bucks County Historical Society.)

"Crossing Watchman" reads the sign on the canal watchmen's booths at Coryell Street in Lambertville. In this busy warehouse and commercial district it was important to keep an eye on business and property and to monitor the safety of pedestrians around the canal. (Photograph courtesy of Yvonne Warren.)

An empty canal boat was easily pulled by the mules. This boat has passed through the manufacturing sections of Lambertville and is moving north to be reloaded upriver, possibly at Frenchtown or Milford. (Photograph courtesy of Yvonne Warren.)

A wonderful J.A. Anderson photograph of a canal boatman relaxing at the end of a long day's journey from New Hope to Point Pleasant. (Photograph courtesy of the Spruance Library at the Bucks County Historical Society.)

Four
Railroads and Trolleys

Billy McCartney worked for the New Hope Post Office. As part of his daily routine, he would walk across the bridge to Lambertville, where he would gather the New Hope mail that had arrived on the Belvidere Delaware Railroad and return to New Hope with it. Mr. McCartney would make this trip twice a day. In this photograph, taken at about the time of World War I, we see him outside the Lambertville Depot. (Photograph courtesy of James Magill.)

Technology emerges in an evolutionary fashion; early inventions or methods give way to improved designs or approaches as demand dictates. Just as the ferry services in the Lambertville and New Hope area gave way to the covered bridge as a means of transportation, canals soon gave way to railroads. Canals and even steamboats represented the primary means of transportation until the mid-nineteenth century, when the speed and relatively low cost of railroads meant that this method of transportation overtook all others.

As was the case in the industrialized nations of Europe, railroads in the U.S. were developed first as a means of transporting goods and supporting heavy industry, with passenger services following as popular, but often unprofitable, operations. In March 1836 the Belvidere Delaware Railroad Company, known as the Bel-Del, was incorporated with the stipulation that the charter was to expire if the railroad was not completed within ten years. An extension of five years was then allowed due to the depression of 1837. In 1847, the Bel-Del project was given a great boost by an infusion of funds from the Hewitt and Cooper Iron Mills in Trenton. At the time, Hewitt and Cooper was one of only five companies in the U.S. that mined iron ore and manufactured the finished project. The owners sponsored the Bel-Del project because they decided that the company would benefit from improved overland transportation.

Passenger service on the Belvidere Delaware Railroad began on February 5, 1851, following the completion of the 14.5-mile section between Trenton and Lambertville. The running time for the trip was about forty minutes, and two return excursions were offered at a cost of 25¢. Robert Fleming served as the engineer on this historic first train. The passenger trains were used for this route until the Pennsylvania Railroad's lease took effect in 1876. Indeed, rail service was highly utilized in this period: in 1874 for instance, well over four hundred thousand passengers were carried on Bel-Del trains. It is difficult to understand now just how astounding and impressive the trains were. Until the railroad was developed, people traveled by foot, by horse-drawn carriages, or by boat, and none of these were particularly fast or comfortable. Part of what drew people to the trains was their speed. One Bel-Del train, known as the "Water Gap Express," became the fastest train in the state of New Jersey by covering the 68 miles of the Bel-Del line in one hour and fifty minutes.

From the 1920s through the 1950s, the Pennsylvania Railroad lobbied for the elimination of passenger service on the Bel-Del. The motivation behind this was an effort to maximize profits by focusing on the highly-profitable freight service on that line. Residents along the line and their political representatives successfully battled the

Pennslyvania Railroad for years in order to maintain passenger service in the community. However, in September 1960, the forces of "profits before people" finally had their way. On October 26, 1960, the last scheduled passenger train ran north on the Bel-Del line carrying only four passengers. When the train entered Union Square in Phillipsburg, only three people were on hand to greet it and offer a tribute to the Belvidere Delaware Railroad's 109 years of passenger service. This stood in contrast to the sound of the cannons, the church bells, and the cheers of thousands that filled the air when the first Bel-Del passenger train arrived in that location in 1854.

In July 1848, J.A. Anderson began working for a team of engineers supervised by Martin Coryell, an assistant to Chief Engineer Ashbel Welch. A great many of the high-quality photographs and daguerreotypes in this book were taken by Anderson, an amateur, yet extremely talented, photographer. In 1886 his religious convictions caused him to resign his position as superintendent of the railroad because it seemed inevitable that the railroad would begin to operate trains on Sundays.

In the 1840s, just before the Bel-Del got off the ground, the Philadelphia and Reading Railroad began operations. Later to be called the Reading Railroad, this company controlled most of the transportation of anthracite. The branch of the Philadelphia and Reading Railroad which began service in New Hope in 1891 was the Northeastern Railroad. Also known as the North Pennsylvania Railroad, this rail service had a considerable edge over the Bel-Del as it also provided service to Philadelphia. The first train to the state capital ran on April 6, 1891, and reduced the trip by 15 miles; in doing so, it made it only too clear that the Bel-Del was no longer the only show in town.

Another newcomer for the Belvidere Delaware Railroad to reckon with was the Pennsylvania and New Jersey Traction Company. In the early 1900s, this trolley line was in direct competition with the Bel-Del in offering passenger service between Lambertville and Trenton. The Traction Company's cars began in Trenton, crossed over the Delaware River to Morrisville, Pennsylvania, and traveled north along the river into New Hope, where they crossed the steel bridge (which replaced the covered bridge lost in the Great Flood of 1903) to Lambertville. This bi-state route allowed for very personalized local service as fifteen to twenty runs were made in each direction every day. Despite the fact that its service was offered at a very reasonable price, the Pennsylvania and New Jersey Traction Company was forced to cease operations in 1924. It simply could not compete with America's new love: the family automobile.

This magnificent photograph, taken south of Lambertville, contains many things of historical importance. We can see, from right to left: the railroad bridge crossing the canal; the Feeder Canal, which was responsible for so much of the early transport of goods; a Bel-Del locomotive

pulling a passenger train south to Trenton; the rapids at Wells Falls; the covered bridge crossing over to Pennsylvania; and the tower of the New Hope-Lumberville United Methodist Church. (Photograph courtesy of Lambertville Historical Society.)

The first train to New Hope ran in 1891. The Philadelphia and Reading Railroad provided much quicker service to Philadelphia than the Bel-Del across the river. Because it covered 15 miles less it was able to garner a considerable number of the Bel-Del's passengers for the trip to the Reading Terminal in Philadelphia. Cyrus Yerkes lived on Bridge Street in New Hope and served as the conductor on the inaugural train. He is the man with his hands folded, standing proudly in front of the train. (Photograph courtesy of James Magill.)

The color of the Reading Depot in New Hope was and still is "Philadelphia Brown." Distinctive pointed roofs like this one could be seen on the Reading depots all along the rail line. This cute little station looks as if it might have been taken from a child's model railroad set. The Ivyland & New Hope trackage was placed back in service as a tourist line in 1965. (Photograph courtesy of James Magill.)

The turntable at Lambertville was used to transfer engines from track to track, and to pull them in for repair and maintenance. The first locomotive built in the shop, the Pequest, was completed in 1864. The engine was painted and gilded by William B. Niece under the foremanship of James Lyons. Many engines were manufactured in this Lambertville shop, including Hercules and Ironsides, but one of the first to run on the Bel-Del Railroad was manufactured by Baldwin Brothers of Philadelphia. (Photograph courtesy of George Kline.)

The new Lambertville Depot was heralded in the *Daily State Gazette* as: "One of the most substantial depots on the Bel-Del." But this handsome, functional, three-story sandstone building barely survived its first year. During the evening of July 10, 1874, a blinding bolt of lightning struck the weather vane on the cupola of the depot. Although the fire was soon extinguished, there was considerable damage to both the cupola and the roof. The depot has now been beautifully restored and currently houses a restaurant. (Photograph courtesy of George Kline.)

There are always many stories—from the romantic to the hair-raising—about rail lines and the people that operate them. One such story tells of a engineer on a eastbound train, who, on a clear night in 1855, was startled by the sudden appearance of a bright light fast approaching him. Fearing a collision with an oncoming locomotive the engineer leaped from his cab. The light turned out to be the full moon rising over the horizon. (Photograph courtesy of Lambertville Historical Society.)

By 1907 most railroad shop workers employed at the Lambertville shops had been transferred to Pennslyvania Railroad shops in Trenton and Morrisville. Although the company initially soothed public sentiment by indicating that it had plans for the "renovation" of the Lambertville Depot, the carpenter shops and roundhouse slowly became targets for demolition. (Photograph courtesy of Lambertville Historical Society.)

The Bel-Del roundhouse is shown here with its turntable and a number of workers. In July 1877, Superintendent J.A. Anderson issued the following memo to his managers: "Foremen and others who employ men in the different departments, are expected to secure those of correct personal character and habits. Those who spend time and money in drinking places, or addicted to other idle and immoral practices, are less able to render good services than sober and moral men, and safety and economy require that they should not be employed." (Photograph courtesy of Lambertville Historical Society.)

The all-weather watchman's shanty on the canal side of the two tracks at Coryell Street in Lambertville is shown here about 1900. This little building is a good example of paneled-board and batten-style construction. Batten down the hatches indeed, because the watchman's job could be a dangerous one. At 1:10 am on February 19, 1910, a Pennsylvania and Reading engine blew up at the New Hope Depot. The locomotive was shattered and a nearby building was destroyed. The explosion was felt throughout New Hope and even in Lambertville. (Photograph courtesy of the Spruance Library at the Bucks County Historical Society.)

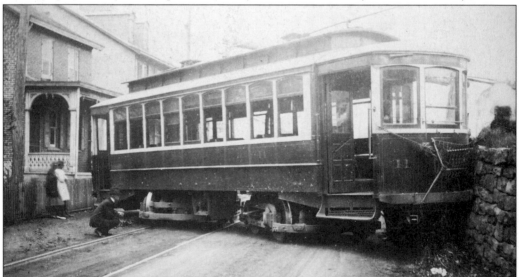

This trolley has somehow come off the track in New Hope. This type of occasional mishap was part of the price paid for using "cutting-edge" technology. The price for a complete trip to Trenton was never more than 36¢ throughout the entire life of the Traction Company—so perhaps it was worth the small risk. Trolley cars such as this were equipped with a pot-belly stove to warm the passengers in cold weather. (Photograph courtesy of James Magill.)

This is the first trolley car run by the Pennsylvania and New Jersey Traction Company entering Lambertville on June 14, 1905. It had carried its passengers all the way from Trenton. The many trips made per day, and the reasonable price of trolley car excursions, made travel between Hunterdon and Mercer Counties in New Jersey and Bucks County in Pennsylvania affordable and convenient. (Photograph courtesy of George Kline.)

At end of what was also known as the "Lambertville Tramline," the trolley car reversed direction and crossed over to New Hope for the return trip south to Trenton. Because the Pennsylvania Railroad refused to permit cars belonging to this "foreign" rail service to cross its tracks, the short distance the trolley traveled in Lambertville up to the PRR tracks has been coined "the shortest trolley route" in the United States. (Photograph courtesy of George Kline.)

It is mid-morning on a warm summer day. The mist has not quite burned off the river, yet the young lovers are setting out for some quiet moments together on the Delaware. The young woman, every bit a young lady, holds her parasol, while her gallant suitor prepares to guide their boat into the calm waters. (Photograph courtesy of George Kline.)

Five
Beautiful Buildings

The first families in Lambertville were the Holcombes (who arrived in 1705) and the Coryells (who came in 1732). This is the Holcombe Farmstead, a house that was home to at least eight generations. General George Washington made the Holcombe Farmstead his local headquarters. Over the years, there were additions to the original stone building, but it is still recognized as an historic farmstead. (Photograph courtesy of Lambertville Historical Society.)

Among the many wonderful things about the Lambertville and New Hope area is that a number of the Victorian and Federal-style buildings remain intact. New Hope has always flourished as a center of commerce and in the early twentieth century it transformed itself into an artist community of considerable renown and has attracted tourists since. Lambertville, on the other hand, evolved very slowly from an industrial city to become the quaint center of antique shops, art galleries, and restaurants that it is today. In recent years both have flourished together and are well known as lovely places to visit. Part of the reason for this is the culture the area has to offer: the art, the antiques, the music, the fine food, and, not the least, the history.

A community's buildings are often a wonderful testimony to its history, and this is certainly the case in both Lambertville and New Hope. Many of the twin river hamlets' wonderful old commercial and residential buildings have been lost to fire, flood, and the human folly that results in gas stations replacing grand old mansions and other structures, but many remain, and it is certain that the knowledge of what has been lost will heighten awareness of the importance of preservation efforts.

When one examines the original buildings of Lambertville and New Hope, it becomes evident that they were designed chiefly with utility and function in mind. Residents needed basic and solid housing to be comfortable and tolerable in both the warm, humid summers and the cold, bitter winters. These buildings were practical and simple in construction, as shown by the basic rectangular windows and chimneys that were built within the wall structure to provide additional support.

The originals dwellings were "vernacular" in that the materials used in construction were limited to what was available in the immediate environment. The Delaware River Valley provided an ample supply of hard and soft wood trees for structural beams and siding. In fact, so much northern yellow pine was used in the construction of early settlements that the trees were milled out of existence. The local hillsides and quarries provided clay for making bricks and the river and neighboring fields provided a large supply of stones thanks to the glaciers that came through in millennia past.

In the mid-seventeenth century, European colonists utilized the relatively safe point where the twin river hamlets stand today to cross the Delaware before heading further west. Thus the very early homes in the area (dating from the 1700s through the early 1800s) are considered Colonial, or Federal, homes. As the "root" style for the structures that were built, the Colonial style was never lost over the years. With each advancing decade new generations built additions or added facades onto the original Colonial structures, thus altering, but never completely losing, the style.

With industrialization in the nineteenth century and the improvements in transportation that went with it, Lambertville and New Hope were transformed from small villages to large towns. The architecture of buildings from this period and the volume in which they were constructed reflect this new world and the prosperity that it engendered. Many of the large Italianate homes that remain standing to this day were constructed during the rich times of the 1850s and 1860s, while the streets lined with workers' houses are testimony to the huge numbers of people arriving to work in the mills and factories.

The prosperity of the late Victorian era, and the increase in disposable income among middle-class families, was responsible in part for the elaborate additions—such as "gingerbread" decoration— made to homes. In the 1880s, the beautiful and ornate Queen Anne and Victorian styles emerged as new architectural fashion statements. Although some of the wonderful mansions that the old-timers remember have been lost to "progress," a casual stroll down many of the twin river hamlets' streets will allow one to see Colonial, Federal, Italianate, Queen Anne, and Victorian buildings sitting side by side.

The Lambert family was among the first families to settle in this area. This is John Lambert's home, "Seabrook," which was named after his bride's family. He was one of the many Lamberts named John: there was a John in every generation. Although the house is no longer owned by descendants of the Lambert family, the property is still as lovely as ever. (Photograph courtesy of the Spruance Library at the Bucks County Historical Society.)

This is the home of John Lambert's father, Gershon Lambert. Gershon Lambert was a local merchant who held important positions in the community as well as serving in the U.S. House of Representatives and the U.S. Senate. It is interesting to note that a tiny fishing village in New Brunswick, Canada, bears the name "Lambertville" after a certain John Lambert of New Jersey settled there soon after the surrender of Lord Cornwallis to General Washington. It is unclear whether the flood of thousands of Tory sympathizers to Canada shortly after the surrender was a mere coincidence. (Photograph courtesy of the Spruance Library at the Bucks County Historical Society.)

The James Wilson Marshall Museum is home to the Lambertville Historical Society. In this photograph we can see the Sisters of Mercy Convent. The convent was at one time added on to the rear of the building, but it has since been removed. The Marshall House is maintained in excellent physical and accurate historical condition by the volunteers of the Lambertville Historical Society. (Photograph courtesy of Lambertville Historical Society.)

This stone structure on Franklin Street in Lambertville is the building that Dr. John Lilly used as a hospital to quarantine patients with "Asiatic cholera" during the construction of the Delaware and Raritan Feeder Canal. This simple stone building has four levels, which was very unusual at the time it was built. River towns were typically built only as high as their surrounding hills, but in this case, part of the hillside was actually used for the earthen walls on the lower level. (Photograph courtesy of the Spruance Library at the Bucks County Historical Society.)

The New Hope Post Office was located at the corner of Bridge and Main Streets. This is where Billy McCartney would return from his twice daily walks to Lambertville to pick up the New Hope mail. It was sorted here, and then distributed to New Hope residents. (Photograph courtesy of James Magill.)

New Hope's first high school was built c. 1870. In 1931, the last class to be taught there, a class of thirteen students, graduated before a new school was constructed. During its days as a functioning school, it housed every student in every grade from first grade through the first two years of high school. Up until 1929, New Hope students interested in pursuing the final two years of high school had to travel either to Doylestown or across the river to Lambertville. For many, the latter school was out of reach because tuition had to be paid. (Photograph courtesy of James Magill.)

In the mid-nineteenth century Lambertville's city fathers recognized the need to expand the city's educational facilities to meet the needs of its youth. Lambertville's first high school was constructed here on the rise of Lambert's Hill. As Lambertville grew, it stretched its borders to the limitations imposed by nature. (Photograph courtesy of Roy Ewing.)

As Lambertville's population grew, the Lambertville High School was expanded to house increasing numbers of students. As time went on, the school building became not merely functional, but more ornate; this was probably a reflection of the increasing prosperity of the village. (Photograph courtesy of Lambertville Historical Society.)

This photograph of the Lambertville High School was taken from Coryell Street. As you can see, attending the high school required a rigorous climb up Lambert's Hill to get to class. Could these forced marches up to school account in part for the athletic prowess demonstrated in the community over the years? (Photograph courtesy of Roy Ewing.)

The Van Dolan School is an example of the octagonal buildings popular in the 1850s, 1860s, and 1870s. Although there are only several hundred examples of this style still in existence in the United States, octagonal buildings were considered at the time to be superior to traditional square houses because they cost less to build and less to heat, and because they allowed increased sunlight and fresh air to enter. (Photograph courtesy of the Spruance Library at the Bucks County Historical Society.)

The Lambertville House was built to serve increased numbers of travelers after legislation passed in 1812 resulted in the construction of a covered bridge at this site to replace the ferry service. Originally a small stone tavern and inn, by the 1880s the Lambertville House was a much larger building with a stucco exterior. (Photograph courtesy of George Kline.)

The Lambertville Masonic Building is a commercial structure that has housed a wide variety of businesses over the years. The first public library (the Stryker Library), Lambertville City Hall, a bank, and several restaurants have all called this building home. Designed by noted Philadelphia architect Samuel Sloan, and built in 1878, the Masonic Building combines several architectural motifs in one composition. It currently houses a variety of businesses, and the Masonic meeting rooms are still in use on the third floor. (Photograph courtesy of Lambertville Historical Society.)

The Lilly Mansion is a wonderfully eclectic mixture of architectural styles. The original house was built in 1812 by Dr. John Lilly. In its heyday the sweeping front lawn was ringed by an ornate iron fence. This mansion and the towering Queen Anne that sat across the street (the current site of a gas station) were the buildings that newcomers to the village would see first. In the 1930s, highway construction claimed part of the mansion's side property and in the 1950s the mansion lost its front lawn to yet another gas station. Fortunately, the Lambertville Public Library is now housed in the Lilly Mansion and great efforts have been made to restore its charm from yesteryear. (Photograph courtesy of Lambertville Historical Society.)

In this view, we see a row of commercial buildings on Bridge Street in New Hope that continue to operate as retail establishments. The oyster house on the left provided an alternative choice for dining for those staying across the street at the inn. As is so often the case in towns that act as transportation hubs, inns and hotels sprung up on either side of the ferries and bridges of Lambertville and New Hope. Note the steel girders on the bridge that was built between Lambertville and New Hope after the Great Flood of 1903. (Photograph courtesy of James Magill.)

This nineteenth-century frame house was the residence and office of Dr. John A. Flood, for years the dentist for most of the residents of New Hope. A Catholic Irishman, Flood was a lifelong Democrat who alternated with Roscoe Conkling Magill, a Quaker and a lifelong Republican, in serving as mayor of New Hope.(It is interesting to note that a Mr. Skillman, much like perennial presidential candidate Wendel Wilkie, always opposed Dr. Flood in the primary; like Wilkie, Skillman never prevailed.) Flood and Magill each held office for three separate terms. The current mayor of New Hope is yet another Magill: Roscoe's son, Jim. (Photograph courtesy of the Spruance Library at the Bucks County Historical Society.)

The construction of this eighteen-room stone mansion was begun in 1867 by William Cowin, who was at that time the mayor of Lambertville. This outstanding example of Tuscan Revival architecture includes a carriage portico, a three-story tower, a "widow's watch," and elegant porches and cornices. (Photograph courtesy of Harold Wireman.)

The Cottage Hill Mansions overlook the community of Lambertville. In many industrial towns, the mill owners and prominent businessmen built their houses on the highest ground in town to escape any foul odors that resulted from various industries and to establish themselves as superiors to the hoipolloi below. These mansions are wonderful examples of Victorian-style

architecture with their gingerbread trim, their towers, and their Italianate windows. The Cottage Hill Mansions have been described as "birds on a wire" because of their beautiful appearance when one looked up at them from the town below. (Photograph courtesy of Joseph Cavallaro.)

Albert Anderson's house is a good example of high-style Victorian architecture. The detail in the cutout work of the trim is particularly good. The pent, the decorative wood fill-in at the top of the gable, and the tower are typical of a grand Victorian house. Albert was the son of the famous photographer J.A. Anderson, who lived just down the street. (Photograph courtesy of the Spruance Library at the Bucks County Historical Society.)

The Lambertville City Hall is an excellent example of French Second Empire architecture. Note the concave and convex slate mansard roof, the pointed hoods on the windows of the tower, and the precise stonework. The building was constructed for A.H. Holcombe in 1870 and deeded to Lambertville in 1949. It is a testament to modern society's emphasis on function over form that the lovely front porch (which was also quite functional) did not survive the transition. (Photograph courtesy of Lambertville Historical Society.)

J.A. Anderson's house on North Union Street in Lambertville was built in 1872 by contractor Fred Parker. This magnificent stone structure was built in Italianate Second Empire style. John A. Anderson was a brilliant and adventurous man who, like Thomas Jefferson, had many diverse interests and was a master of several skills. Although photography was just a hobby, he was very proficient in this area—as many of his photographs in this book attest. (Photograph courtesy of the Spruance Library at the Bucks County Historical Society.)

The Elgin House is a picturesque two-and-a-half-story brick Italianate structure with a Queen Anne tower. Note the conical roof, flared walls, and fish-scale shingles. Historical records indicate that Gershon Lambert built the house around 1860. William Smith of Lambertville's Smith & Sons Wire Company lived here from 1902 to 1917, and the house remained in his family until 1929. (Photograph courtesy of James Mastrich and Kathryn Hall.)

The York Street House, built in 1909, was Lambertville's first Neo-Georgian structure. The house was built by local coal and wood entrepreneur George W. Massey as a wedding anniversary gift for his wife. It was designed by Philadelphia architects Schemmerhorn and Wilson, and was featured on the cover of a 1911 edition of *Home and Garden* magazine. Among its many interesting details are: fireplaces with handmade Mercer tiles from Doylestown, Pennsylvania; a Waterford chandelier; half-gas/half-electric light fixtures; and a central vacuum cleaner system dating from 1911. (Photograph courtesy of James Mastrich and Kathryn Hall.)

In 1879, the facade, windows, and roof line of the Conover and Conover mercantile building were redesigned. Before these renovations, the 1846 gabled building had large plate-glass windows and a classical mercantile shade extending over the sidewalk. The alterations were made to a much more sophisticated, eclectic design reminiscent of the work of noted Philadelphia architect Frank Furness. The building is still a commercial property housing a number of different businesses. (Photograph courtesy of James Mastrich and Kathryn Hall.)

The Parry Mansion was originally constructed in 1784. It is a wonderful example of the way Federal-style buildings were eventually adorned with architectural decorations. The dentils, grand brackets, and other lovely details are testimony to the fact that New Hope had moved on from being a frontier town to becoming an established and prosperous community. (Photograph courtesy of George Kline.)

The Huffnagle Mansion is a grand house located in a lovely wooded section of New Hope. When it was built, *c.* 1820, it was known as Springdale. Of all the Huffnagle family members, Dr. Charles Huffnagle is the most well known. He spent a good deal of time overseas working with the East India Company and then as a career officer in the Foreign Service. In 1857, Dr. Huffnagle was appointed by President Polk to the position of First Consul to British India. On each visit to Springdale, Dr. Huffnagle added to his highly-regarded collection of important paintings and curios. (Photograph courtesy of James Magill.)

This is a 1890 photograph of the Leiby Mansion on South Main Street in New Hope. The house, constructed in French Second Empire style, was built by tack and livery store owner Charles Crook in 1865 as a gift for his wife. The building was subsequently home and office to Dr. Kenneth Leiby, who delivered most of the babies in New Hope. When Dr. Leiby decided to sell the building, his only condition was that the owner must "preserve the integrity of the house and my favorite tree." His terms have been honored and the mansion is currently a bed and breakfast lodging. (Photograph courtesy of the Mansion Inn.)

Six

Floods and Fires

This view, looking across the Delaware to New Hope, shows the covered bridge, a railroad building in the foreground, and the New Hope-Lumberville United Methodist Church to the left. Note the sparsity of mature trees in the hills overlooking New Hope: by this time the original virgin forests had been used by generations of settlers for building and heating to the point that the hillsides were quite barren. (Photograph courtesy of George Kline.)

Between Lambertville and New Hope lies the Delaware River. While the river separates the twin river hamlets, it has also represented an immutable connection between them for as long as the two settlements have been in existence. The Delaware has always been, and continues to be, the lifeblood of both towns. Yet it is a force to be reckoned with, because it is just as capable of taking life as giving it. In this chapter we will look more closely at how it binds the two communities together, and how they have joined together in times of celebration and in times of crisis.

Ferry service across the Delaware River between Lambertville and New Hope was essential to the development of these two hamlets. Since at least the 1730s, people, their horses, and their supplies have been transported across the Delaware River. When the first bridge was completed in January 1814, Lambertville and New Hope expanded exponentially. While working men had always crossed the river by necessity, entire families were now able to make the crossing with ease, and travel through the area to destinations farther afield was made much easier. Most residents and travelers were only too happy to avail themselves of the new bridge and had little time to regret the passing of the old days; but there were, however, dangers ahead.

In the evening of October 9 and the early morning of October 10, 1903, the river crested in the Lambertville and New Hope area during one of the most destructive floods ever experienced in the Delaware Valley. A record 11.5 inches of rain fell over the area in a 24-hour period and ten bridges between Belvidere and Trenton were either severely damaged or completely washed away. Upriver at Easton, the river rose to over 40 feet. It was reported in a local newspaper that the tracks of the Belvidere Division of the Pennsylvania Railroad, just above the Alexauken Creek outlet in Lambertville, "looked like a twisted corkscrew stretched across a ditch where the embankment should have been." In fact, the flood caused serious damage to the entire Bel-Del system and the railroad's planing and woodworking mills in Lambertville were completely flooded, causing extensive damage to the machinery.

The Great Flood of 1903 hit Lambertville and New Hope so hard that the devastation is still retold in local folklore. The unfortunate demise of William LaFever is but one tragedy of the Great Flood. This good Samaritan volunteered to row out into the swirling waters to help take a friend from Lumberville to his job at Raven Rock. As soon as he entered the Delaware, his boat was struck by a house that was floating downstream, and the boat capsized. Just as they had in the past, and would again in the future, the two communities pulled together to repair the damage and rebuild homes and businesses.

The people of Lambertville and New Hope also came to each other's aid when fire threatened. Rather than letting buildings and property go up in smoke and risking an entire town, fire companies from both sides of the river can to this day be seen streaking over the bridge to help put out the flames just as they did in days gone by.

Early residents and business owners knew the importance of responding to fires as quickly as possible. Because homes and factories were often very close together, a fire in one put the other in great danger. Factory owners would address the threat of fire by preparing buckets of sand and water and other firefighting equipment so that they would be ready if a fire broke out. The residents of Lambertville and New Hope also recognized the threat that fire posed to their homes and loved ones and so from the inception of organized firefighting in both towns the fire companies have always been staffed by willing and loyal volunteers. It was in everyone's interest to take the risk of fire very seriously.

The Eagle Fire Company of New Hope was for many years the only fire company for both villages. "The Eagle," as it was known, was officially incorporated in the 1860s, but it operated as an organized unit as early as 1812. It is the oldest fire company in Bucks County and among the first fire companies in the nation.

Like New Hope, Lambertville had a few basic firefighting efforts long before fire companies were officially incorporated. Among the first companies in Lambertville was the Aquetong Fire Company, which was formed in 1863. It was joined soon after by the Union Fire Company, the Fleet Wing Hook and Ladder Company, the Hibernia Fire Company (with its kelly green engine), and the Columbia Fire Company. The latter four are still in operation. The towns were saved many times by the combined efforts of all the fire companies. There has always been a spirit of cooperation among the fire departments and they consider themselves to be "sister" companies.

While most of the many fires experienced by Lambertville and New Hope have been held under control, there have also been ones that simply got away, such as the 1860 fire at the India Rubber Company and 1896 breakout at the Lambertville Rubber Company. The excitement and drama of fires and floods meant that many photographers, amateur and professional alike, tried to capture them on film. As a result, many towns have tremendous archives of images of fires and floods. While it might be argued that these images look alike, despite their drama, they are crucial to the telling of history as they preserve the appearance of certain buildings or scenes that might otherwise be lost forever.

In this stereographic view of the covered bridge looking from Lambertville we can see the toll collector's station on the left. Stereographs were cards with two small, identical images set side by side. When one looked at the card through special viewing glasses, a 3-D image was created. Note the wagon ruts in the streets leading to the bridge. The ferry continued in operation for a while after the opening of the bridge because the Conestoga wagons could not fit in the covered bridge and because horses sometimes refused to cross bridges. (Photograph courtesy of Joseph Cavallaro.)

This winter scene shows the covered bridge and part of New Hope. The Delaware River has iced over many times. In January 1866, the *Lambertville Beacon* recorded that with the Delaware completely frozen over, people were driving their sleds and wagons onto the thick ice coating the river to avoid the bridge tolls. (Photograph courtesy of the Spruance Library at the Bucks County Historical Society.)

J.A. Anderson stood out on the frozen Delaware River to take this photograph. The winters in this area were once known for their severity; during the winter of 1696–97, the river was frozen over for three entire months. It was recorded that sleighs and sleds passed freely over the thick ice as far downriver as Philadelphia. In this view, taken looking south, the slope of Goat Hill in Lambertville can be seen to the right of the photograph, under the bridge. (Photograph courtesy of the Spruance Library at the Bucks County Historical Society.)

The 1814 covered bridge at Stockton, New Jersey, stood just 3 miles north of the twin river hamlets. It was damaged by the Great Flood of 1903 and then destroyed in 1923 by a fire caused by lightening. Stockton was originally called Center Bridge, but the name was changed (in honor of Senator Stockton) to avoid confusion with Center Bridge, the little village in Pennsylvania directly just across the Delaware. (Photograph courtesy of George Kline.)

This photograph shows the rapidly rising waters of the Great Flood of 1903 about to destroy the covered bridge in Washington Crossing. After the bridge was rebuilt in 1905, the cost to cross the bridge was 2¢ on foot, 4¢ if pushing a wheelbarrow, and if one was mounted on horse or mule, the cost soared to 10¢. (Photograph courtesy of George Kline.)

This photograph, taken on October 9, 1903, shows the rising water of the Delaware River at New Hope and Lambertville as it reached the level of the bridge. The bridge would be lost the next morning. Previous to this, it had survived, albeit with damage, several floods. It is thought that one bridge piling that has the appearance of a "cow catcher" was repaired in that manner after a piece of an upriver bridge caused severe damage during the Flood of 1841. (Photograph courtesy of George Kline.)

This photograph shows the residents of Lambertville gathering south of the Belvidere Delaware Railroad Depot to watch the disaster that is about to happen as the river continues to rise. The bridge was lost soon thereafter. (Photograph courtesy of George Kline.)

The Delaware House at the corner of Bridge and Main Street in New Hope was the first stop for food and lodging as travelers crossed the covered bridge from Lambertville. In this photograph taken during the Flood of 1903, the inn's guests join area residents in assessing the flood damage. (Photograph courtesy of James Magill.)

The broken bridge is shown here in a view from Lambertville. The entire bridge was swept downriver with the exception of this torn section on the Lambertville side. (Photograph courtesy of James Magill.)

This photograph shows the collapsed entryway on the New Hope side of the bridge. The current is more swift along the Pennsylvania side of the Delaware and this probably accounts for the severity of the damage on this side of the river. (Photograph courtesy of James Magill.)

This section of the ravaged bridge was washed a few miles downriver in the flood waters and appears to have landed across from Bowman's Hill in New Jersey. The torrent of water sweeping downstream literally tore it from the piece that remained on the Lambertville side. A story is told of how the oil lamps on the torn bridge remained burning, illuminating the disaster as it slipped downriver. No doubt it was a very eerie scene. (Photograph courtesy of James Magill.)

A muddle of stones was all that was left of the covered bridge pilings after the flood. The steel bridge that was built as a replacement is now home to cliff swallows that return every year. They were once near extinction, but, realizing that they were about to lose another local treasure, Lambertville and New Hope townspeople lured them back by means of artificial nests placed underneath the bridge. They now herald the arrival of spring in great numbers. (Photograph courtesy of George Kline.)

The construction of the steel bridge that replaced the covered bridge was completed in 1904. The north side of the bridge was reinforced in order to withstand the weight of the trolleys operated by the Pennsylvania and New Jersey Traction Company. Two years after the covered bridge was lost, the first trolley crossed the bridge from New Hope to Lambertville. (Photograph courtesy of Lambertville Historical Society.)

Perseverance Mill was located on the east bank of the Feeder Canal in Lambertville. It was built in 1879 by Mr. McCready, who named it Perseverance Mill because several enterprises that he had owned in the past had burned down, and he was determined to continue in business. Unfortunately, this October 20, 1922 photograph shows the perseverance of fire. After Perseverance Mill I was destroyed, McCready rebuilt the mill on the south side of town and called it Perseverance Mill II. (Photograph courtesy of George Kline.)

On December 27, 1903, the year of the Great Flood, Lambertville suffered yet another tragedy with a fire in the Hooker Building. The tower and the top floor of the building were never replaced, and as the abandoned building slowly deteriorated, the upper floors were all removed until it was eventually reduced to the one-story building that we know today. The cause of the fire remains a charred mystery. (Photograph courtesy of George Kline.)

On February 5, 1912, the New Hope Post Office caught fire. Men that were with the Eagle Fire Company at the time remember that it was so bitterly cold that day that the hoses carrying water from the Delaware River became frozen solid. As a consequence, nothing could be done to prevent the building from burning. Rumors circulated about the cause: the most popular one was that, in an effort to keep warm, someone overheated a coal stove. Three days earlier the Malloy Building in Lambertville had caught fire. In both cases, the "sister" fire companies joined together to face the crises. (Photograph courtesy of George Kline.)

The Union Fire Company was located on Church Street in Lambertville. "The Union" was one of the first firefighting companies in Lambertville to have horse-drawn equipment and a hand pump. Its first "steamer" was purchased in 1891 and it proved to be a very effective engine. Throughout the later decades of the nineteenth century, the equipment and leadership of the fire companies in Lambertville were said to "compare favorably with any town of its size." (Photograph courtesy of George Kline.)

In New Hope, the volunteer firefighters would carry their hoses on horse-drawn carriages like as this one, belonging to the Eagle Fire Company. This company was known as the Delaware Fire Company from approximately 1822 until 1864, when a hand pumper was purchased from the Eagle Fire Company of Trenton. (Photograph courtesy of the Spruance Library at the Bucks County Historical Society.)

The Eagle Fire Company's first motorized automatic pumper engine was purchased in 1920. The water pumping equipment was manufactured by the Hahn Motor Company of Hamburg, Pennsylvania, and the vehicle was powered by a REO engine. Mr. Ransom E. Olds was the founder of the Oldsmobile company. He had been making automobiles for about twenty years by the time this pumper was manufactured. (Photograph courtesy of James Magill.)

This photograph shows the New Hope Eagle Fire Company in dress uniform. The villages' residents not only responded to fire and other hardships at the local level, but they felt a kinship with those who had suffered tragedy in the outside world. In 1871, every employee of the Bel-Del Railroad shops contributed one day's wages for the relief of those who suffered losses in the Great Chicago Fire. The railroad's superintendent, J.A. Anderson, authorized the free shipment of all relief packages for victims of the fire. (Photograph courtesy of James Magill.)

The Fleet Wing Hook and Ladder Company firehouse was built in 1867. The building has Italianate influences, distinctive glasswork in the bay, interesting brackets, and a cornice crowned by a central arch and an ornate cupola. The old horse-drawn hose carriage inside the building represented a major technological advance: in the 1840s hose carts were pulled by shifts of volunteers in order to siphon water from the canal for fighting fires. (Photograph courtesy of George Kline.)

Some families in New Hope and Lambertville have had members from at least three generations serve proudly as volunteer firemen in the towns' fire companies. This is the horse-drawn ladder carriage of the New Hope Eagle Fire Company. (Photograph courtesy of George Kline.)

The Hibernia Fire Company in Lambertville sports both a beautiful fire carriage and building. Here we see admiring children perhaps dreaming of becoming fire fighters. It is said that one reason so many beautiful and interesting buildings remain to this day is the presence of so many fire companies and so many willing volunteers. (Photograph courtesy of Lambertville Historical Society.)

Seven
Churches

A Pennsylvania and New Jersey Traction Company trolley was photographed in front of the New Hope-Lumberville United Methodist Church around the time of the World War I. (Photograph courtesy of George Kline.)

The earliest settlers of the Delaware Valley were a diverse group of immigrants belonging to a number of different religions. Heading west across what was then a vast wilderness, the settlers were English, Scotch-Irish, Dutch, and German in nationality; and Protestant, Catholic, Quaker, and Huguenot in religion. In the seventeenth century, and indeed through to the twentieth, religion was a tremendously important part of every individual's life and of every community, so the settlers formed congregations as soon as there were enough members to support them, and built houses of worship as soon as funds were available. Religious diversity was a keyword across America in these infant communities, and this has continued to the present day. What has changed, however, is the support that churches can expect from the local community, with many churches actually selling their buildings as a response to thinning congregations.

Until recently, however, churches were very much the center of a settlement or community. Church construction and enlargement in the twin river hamlets mirrors the pattern of population growth in the two communities: congregations grew slowly during the first half of the nineteenth century and worshiped in humble buildings, but as the church communities grew, they built larger, and often more majestic, churches and meetinghouses. This area of the Delaware Valley is blessed with a multitude of magnificent churches, many of which are recorded in local, state, and national historical archives.

One particularly interesting story is that of the Mount Moriah African Methodist Episcopal (AME) Church. The congregation was formed in 1818 and when its church building was constructed on West Mechanic Street in 1840, it became the first church of any kind to be erected within the town limits of New Hope. Mount Moriah thrived for a long period of time, but with the shifting demographic patterns that accompanied the Great Depression of the 1930s, it lost many members of its congregation. All that now remains of the church are some gravestones in the backyard of a house on the site where Mount Moriah once stood. However, the African-American church still maintains a presence in the community: the Mount Carmel Baptist Church, built in Lambertville in 1897, continues to be a thriving congregation at 247 North Main Street.

The most important people in the community in the seventeenth, eighteenth, and nineteenth centuries were the local ministers, attorneys, and physicians. These were the figures of spiritual, legal, and physical care that people from all walks of life looked to for leadership and support. Despite the expected class divisions, however, these people mingled with their neighbors at church, and it was the congregation that in many ways brought people together and transcended barriers of wealth and class. To an extent that would surprise many people today, congregations were often almost self-sufficient entities whose members would support each other through good times and bad.

Although the different congregations could be said to work as communities in their own right, the barriers between congregations or faiths were not as high as one might think. A strong demonstration of this spirit of intra-community fellowship was the New Hope Sunday School that the Reverend Peter O. Studdiford took under his wing in 1820. Local residents from all faiths attended Sunday school classes which were focused as much on literacy as on learning from the bible. Quakers, Presbyterians, Methodists, and AME members all gathered and learned together. In bringing these people together, Reverend Studdiford clearly played a pivotal role in the development of church and community life in New Hope and Lambertville. He was so revered, in fact, that at his funeral a procession of thirty clergymen led services packed with more than one thousand of the faithful from both sides of the river. The Belvidere Delaware Railroad even ran a special train to Trenton to bring mourners who were arriving from Philadelphia and New York to the service. In his eulogy famous nineteenth-century theologian Professor Charles Hodge of the Princeton Seminary said: "No man can estimate what it is for a community to have such a man settle among them in their forming period, and to be spared to them for nearly half a century. Generations yet unborn will have reason to bless his name and revere his memory."

Hodge was quite right in his assessment of Studdiford's influence, for churches have remained a cornerstone of life in New Hope and Lambertville. Not only have they helped the towns' leaders find the resolve to make the difficult decisions all leaders must face, but they have also assisted the common person in the search for inner peace. The presence of the church has clearly helped to shape the people who served both communities, and it continues to do so today.

The New Hope-Lumberville United Methodist Church on South Main Street in New Hope was built in 1874. It represents the combined heritage of three area congregations: the New Hope United Methodist Church, the Lumberville United Methodist Church, and the New Hope Presbyterian Churches. The congregation anticipates that they will soon be moving from the existing church building to a more central location in Solebury Township. (Photograph courtesy of New Hope-Lumberville United Methodist Church.)

In 1882, this list of rules was published for the congregation to heed. The "M.E." stands for Methodist Episcopal, which is the former name of the New Hope-Lumberville United Methodist Church. Charles Crook, the prosperous local businessman who built what is now known as the Leiby Mansion, was a leading member of the church for over half a century. He was also a lay preacher. The legend goes that the reason the church did not have a bell installed in its tower until 1975 is that Mr. Crook and his family did not want their quiet disturbed. (Photograph courtesy of New Hope-Lumberville United Methodist Church.)

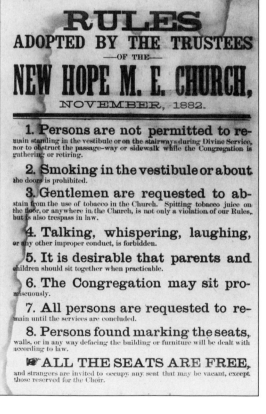

RULES
ADOPTED BY THE TRUSTEES
—OF THE—
NEW HOPE M. E. CHURCH,
NOVEMBER, 1882.

1. **Persons are not permitted to re-**main standing in the vestibule or on the stairways during Divine Service, nor to obstruct the passage-way or sidewalk while the Congregation is gathering or retiring.

2. **Smoking in the vestibule or about** the doors is prohibited.

3. **Gentlemen are requested to ab-**stain from the use of tobacco in the Church. Spitting tobacco juice on the floor, or anywhere in the Church, is not only a violation of our Rules, but is also trespass in law.

4. **Talking, whispering, laughing,** or any other improper conduct, is forbidden.

5. **It is desirable that parents and** children should sit together when practicable.

6. **The Congregation may sit pro-**miscuously.

7. **All persons are requested to re-**main until the services are concluded.

8. **Persons found marking the seats,** walls, or in any way defacing the building or furniture will be dealt with according to law.

☞ **ALL THE SEATS ARE FREE,**
and strangers are invited to occupy any seat that may be vacant, except those reserved for the Choir.

The Centenary Methodist Church at North Main and Jefferson Streets in Lambertville was originally known as the Centenary Methodist Episcopal Church. The church was constructed by Cornelius Arnett, who built numerous commercial and residential buildings in town. This beautiful Romanesque edifice is the congregation's second church; the first was located at 63 Coryell Street. Although the building was constructed in 1865, the congregation did not move into the church until 1866. That year marked a century of organized worship by the Methodist Church in the United States and so the church was named the Centenary Methodist Church. (Photograph courtesy of George Kline.)

Saint Andrews Episcopal Church in Lambertville has had several homes. It was formed in Ringoes in 1716 and moved to Lambertville in 1835. It is on the site of Captain George Coryell's trading post. Captain Erskine DeWitt, map maker to General Washington, indicated on a map of Coryell's Crossing that the trading post was one of only four buildings in the area at the time of the Revolution. (Photograph courtesy of George Kline.)

Top Left: Reverend Herbert Smith was the son of Reverend Elvin K. Smith, who was the first rector at Saint Andrews. The father and son team is remembered for their care of the dying during the typhoid epidemic of the 1890s. (Photograph courtesy of the Spruance Library at the Bucks County Historical Society.)

Top Right: Saint Andrews Episcopal Church was a warm and inviting place in the snow. The Reverends Smith and Smith were quite concerned that their parishioners be enlightened and consequently they did their best to increase the literacy rate of their congregation. (Photograph courtesy of Yvonne Warren.)

The area churches went through cycles of expansion, renovation, and repair. This photograph shows the bell that was about to be installed in the newly-constructed Saint Andrews Episcopal Church in Lambertville being removed from its temporary location. (Photograph courtesy of the Spruance Library at the Bucks County Historical Society.)

Lambertville's first Episcopal church burned in 1891. It remained a shell until it was revitalized as a residence in the 1920s. The original Gothic church windows are preserved in the building, which is in use today as bed and breakfast lodging. (Photograph courtesy of Lambertville Historical Society.)

The First Presbyterian Church is one of several magnificent churches in Lambertville. It is an excellent example of Greek Revival-style architecture with its temple front facade. The church property was donated by the Lamberts and the Coryells as their property line literally split the building in half. In 1817, the church was called the Union Presbyterian Church of Georgetown and Lambertville. (Photograph courtesy of George Kline.)

The Reverend P.O. Studdiford had no intention of settling in the area, but he was quite taken by the calling to minister to the residents. They, in turn were quite taken by him. In 1821, he began preaching at both the Thompson Memorial Church (then called Solebury Church) and the Lambertville Presbyterian Church. He was installed as pastor of the two churches in 1824 and he remained in that position until 1848. At that point he resigned from the Solebury Presbyterian Church so that he could dedicate all of his energy to the Lambertville Church. He once preached before the Marquis de Lafayette in Trenton and was a close friend of Reverend Charles Hodge. (Photograph courtesy of New Hope-Lumberville United Methodist Church.)

The First Presbyterian Church at Flat Iron Point in New Hope was built in 1872. It was originally constructed as the chapel for the New Hope Sunday School, but in 1893, under the leadership of Reverend Wilbur C. Mickey, the congregation was formally organized into the New Hope Presbyterian Church. Services continued at this site until the church building was converted into the New Hope Free Library in the 1970s. (Photograph courtesy of New Hope-Lumberville United Methodist Church.)

Samuel D. Ingham served his country as a congressman and also as President Andrew Jackson's secretary of the treasury. His biographer noted that he was "always a regular attendant on the preaching of the gospel and a firm believer in the fundamental doctrine of Christianity." In November 1817, his wife Rebecca helped him to found the New Hope Female Religious Tract Society and within four months this small band of ladies distributed nearly five hundred pieces of Christian literature. In 1818, the congressman assisted her in founding the New Hope Sunday School. (Photograph courtesy of New Hope-Lumberville United Methodist Church.)

The First Presbyterian Church is the oldest church in Lambertville. When the congregation outgrew the 1817 church, this structure was built on the same site in 1848. Reverend P.O. Studdiford was succeeded by his son P.A. Studdiford as minister of the congregation. It is ironic that between the First Presbyterian Church at the head of Church Street and the original Saint John's Catholic Church at the opposite end stood a mixture of taverns and brothels, giving the street a feel of both heaven and hell. (Photograph courtesy of the Spruance Library at the Bucks County Historical Society.)

The Thompson Memorial Presbyterian Church, formerly the Solebury Presbyterian Church, was built in 1811. The 2 acres that the church sits on were purchased for $40 the year before from Robert T. Neely, who was raised in what is now known as the Thompson-Neely House. For many years, this early church filled the spiritual needs of people on both sides of the river. The beautiful stonework is characteristic of many other Bucks County structures. (Photograph courtesy of New Hope Historical Society.)

The First Baptist Church was built in 1868. It is the second oldest church in Lambertville and is an outstanding example of Romanesque architecture. The interior alone took fourteen years to complete. The cornerstone holds a gold nugget placed in honor of James Marshall, whose family was one of the five that founded the church. Unfortunately, its original corner spires have long since broken off. (Photograph courtesy of George Kline.)

The Saint John the Evangelist Catholic Church was built in Lambertville in 1892. It is an excellent example of Gothic Revival architecture. Father William J. Fitzgerald personally supervised the cutting of locally-quarried Scotch granite blocks and also monitored the progress of construction. The property for Saint John the Evangelist was purchased "quietly" in 1879 to prevent opposition from the Protestant majority in town. It is interesting to note that the stone for the church was rumored to have been secretly donated by two Protestants. (Photograph courtesy of George Kline.)

Saint Martin of Tours Catholic Church was built on a gentle hillside overlooking New Hope in 1885. Saint Martin of Tours was a soldier in the Roman army who became one of the most venerated saints of the Middle Ages. Many of the members of the church's congregation were descendants of the settlers that William Penn recruited from Germany and the British Isles to help develop Pennsylvania. A large number of these people were escaping wars and religious persecution in their native countries. (Photograph courtesy of New Hope Historical Society.)

The first house of worship to be built by white settlers was the 1806 Friends Meeting House in Solebury. The Quakers, also known as the Society of Friends, followed William Penn to Pennsylvania and were the dominant religious group among the settlers in the 1680s. The congregation was affiliated with the Buckingham Friends Meeting House until this building was erected. (Photograph courtesy of the Spruance Library at the Bucks County Historical Society.)

This panoramic view of New Hope and part of Lambertville shows many of the spires and towers of the area's churches. This is visual evidence of the central place that houses of worship held in both villages. (Photograph courtesy of New Hope Historical Society.)

Eight
Lifestyle

Lewis Island in Lambertville has long been used by the public for swimming and other recreational activities. Crowds would swarm to the beach on warm summer afternoons and indulge in the soda and candy floss that was sold there. (Photograph courtesy of George Kline.)

There were, and still are, many colorful aspects of life in New Hope and Lambertville. Music, art, dance, opera, and sports, as well as patriotic, social, literary, and religious clubs, have always been an important part of the fabric of both communities. The Delaware was just as important as a location for play as it was for work and this is the theme that runs through the following images.

In the years before the television revolutionized America's leisure time, people grasped any and all excuses for community get-togethers and parades. It is obvious from the variety of images shown here that the town's folk mingled a great deal and continue to do so by socializing at community events. Fire companies were glad to show off their latest equipment and horses, and later, their trucks and mascots. Bands abounded with good musicians of all ages and concerts were performed frequently for the public. Activities held by church-affiliated organizations filled the calendar and were well attended with everyone dressed in their best bib and tucker.

Both towns enjoyed church and civic events and celebrations, but New Hope had a slightly different focus because of the influence of the artistic community. William L. Lathrop arrived in New Hope in the late 1890s, and, although he could not know it at the time, he was the first in a long line of talented painters who gravitated to New Hope independent of each other, but who together comprised what is known as the New Hope School of Painting. Among these artists were impressionist painter Edward Redfield, whose use of bold colors and broad strokes stood in contrast to Lathrop's style, and Daniel Garber, a realist painter and printmaker. These artists all loved the play of light on the Delaware River and the trees of the surrounding hillsides, and probably enjoyed the sense of community engendered by the close proximity of other artists.

The local people initially found many of the artists quite foreign because they pursued a lifestyle that was very different from their own. However, once the artists and locals began to know each other on a personal level, a mutual respect and understanding developed into a bond that is still felt in the community.

The emphasis on the arts continued to grow over the years. The famous Bucks County Playhouse, located in the old Parry Grist Mill, was visited by many a Broadway star in the summer months and continues to feature an array of acts today. The Lambertville Music Circus was among several other tent theaters that brought together talented performers and enthusiastic audiences. People traveled considerable distances to see these shows and the lodging and restaurant businesses that grew up as a result have evolved into the excellent bed and breakfast and restaurant cottage industry for which Lambertville and New Hope are known today.

There are many examples of the rich fabric of community life in Lambertville and New Hope. J. Fenimore Boozer's approach to holiday celebrating and generosity provides a warm memory. Boozer was the proprietor of a hardware store located on the corner of Union and Coryell Streets in Lambertville. Each Christmas from 1853 through the 1870s he played the part of Father Christmas by giving out hundreds of bags of goodies to more than 1,200 children who visited his store. His heartfelt generosity was returned as he was eventually elected mayor for a term. He was affectionately known to the community as "Uncle Finney."

And, of course, people always seemed to make time in their busy lives for frivolity. An event known as the Great Sleigh Race took place on January 2, 1873. In this contest several of the community's prominent residents threw caution to the wind as they competed in a horse-drawn sleigh race from Lambertville to Center Bridge and back. A similarly riotous event held for many years was the Lambertville Tub Race. In this event, fully grown gentlemen would select a seaworthy wash tub, and race from Delaware Street south to Coryell Street on the Feeder Canal.

Sport was also central to community life. In January 1867, Angel's Ice Skating Rink was first opened to the public. Many an evening was spent dancing across the ice. This state-of-the-art facility was fitted with coal stoves for warmth and featured a separate room for the ladies.

Quite distinct from the grace of ice skating was the pugilism of boxing. It was reported in the *Easton Sentinel* in 1867 that many prize fights took place between competitors from near and far in secluded locations such as Bull's Island. Many a gentleman (and some very ungentlemenly fellows) would take the Bel-Del for the short ride to bet on a fight or just to enjoy the contest. These prize and wager contests were held within a short distance of the Delaware because of a Pennsylvania law which stated that: "The penalty for enjoying a prize fight (in Pennsylvania), or taking part as a second or battle-holder was a fine of more than $1,000, and solitary imprisonment not exceeding two years."

One can never quite capture in words the lifestyle and culture of a community in days gone by. It truly has to be experienced; to be heard, felt, seen, and touched. The following photographs might give you a little taste of what once was. And perhaps if you let your imagination fly, you may be able to understand what it was like to be a resident of the twin river villages in days gone by.

Every April crowds still gather on Lewis Island to watch the shad fishermen pull in their long nets. It was also here that Mabel Shoemaker pulled in her beau and future husband, Jim Warner. After glancing at this photograph seventy years later, Mabel, always a "cut-up," remarked "My! Look at those breasts!" (Photograph courtesy of the Warner Family.)

The Grand Army Post is on the march. Lambertville's many parades are still quite popular, especially the Halloween parade. (Photograph courtesy of the Spruance Library at the Bucks County Historical Society.)

Businesses often sponsored musical groups, such as the Lambertville Cadets, to show that they supported local people and events. They hoped to encourage the community's youth to display good social behavior and community pride. (Photograph courtesy of Lambertville Historical Society.)

The New Hope Home Guard stood ready to come to the aid of the community. Here they are drilling with wooden guns as World War I raged many miles away. (Photograph courtesy of James Magill.)

This scene captures the grandeur of a World War I-era parade on Main Street in New Hope. Lambertville and New Hope people have always been very patriotic: Washington's crossing of the Delaware on his way to glory in Trenton was first remembered by a grand parade in Lambertville in 1878. The guest of honor at that event was Aunt Grace Brittan, who remembered seeing the great general and his army when she was just three years old. (Photograph courtesy of James Magill.)

This squad of football players took a time-out in order to pose in front of the bridge in Lambertville. Another rigorous sport that captured the interest of some was croquet. It was not quite as glamorous as football, and certainly less popular. In September 1873 a reporter announced his opinion of the sport in the *Easton Sentinel*: "Croquet season is over and the stupid and senseless game has been abandoned until next spring." (Photograph courtesy of Lambertville Historical Society.)

116

Tennis certainly had a following at Ely Field. It was not, however, the only game imported from England. Cricket was a popular game that encouraged inter-community competition. It preceded baseball as a local pastime. As early as the July 4, 1859, the Lambertville Cricket Club defeated the Trenton Cricket Club 142 to 127. The following year a second local club, called the Delaware Cricket Club, was founded. (Photograph courtesy of George Kline.)

By the 1860s baseball began to emerge as a popular sport. A local newspaper reported on May 22, 1902, that the Lambertville Athletic Club behind the battery of Vinson and Kline defeated the North Philadelphia Browns 16–1. In this photograph of a baseball game played in Lambertville, we can see an advertisement for the Lambertville Puffs. (Photograph courtesy of George Kline.)

The wooded hillsides by which the communities were bound were filled during the warm weather with girls' and boys' organized groups. A drink from a cool stream and ghost stores told around a campfire were fondly remembered in later years. (Photograph courtesy of Lambertville Historical Society.)

Bicycling was a very popular sport for both men and women, with some taking part in races, and others simply touring the countryside on summer afternoons. This photograph shows William Shoemaker, Ed Fleming, and Bill Morse out for a ride. (Photograph courtesy of the Warner Family.)

Mr. Oblinger, the director of the Union Paper Manufacturing Company in New Hope, took his friends out for a drive for the sheer pleasure of feeling the wind blow through their hair. (Photograph courtesy of James Magill.)

These men are making cider wearing what appears to be their "Sunday best." Perhaps this photograph was taken on a Sunday and the men are posing for the camera rather than actually working. Cider making is still is a major industry in this agricultural area. (Photograph courtesy of the Spruance Library at the Bucks County Historical Society.)

Cutting, splitting, and stacking wood was a job usually assigned to the men. Wood was used for heating the house and as fuel for cooking on the Franklin stove. (Photograph courtesy of Lambertville Historical Society.)

Wells were strategically located in the business and residential sections of town. This well was located on the north side of Coryell Street in Lambertville, between the canal and the river. There are still people in Lambertville who remember drinking the sweet, cold water from the well as children. (Photograph courtesy of the Spruance Library at the Bucks County Historical Society.)

A canal man takes his rest under a spreading shade tree after a hard day's work. This is a time-honored tradition of all working people. (Photograph courtesy of Lambertville Historical Society.)

The last of the many shad fisheries that once lined the Delaware River is located on Lewis Island. The success of the catch is greatly influenced by the warmth of the water as the shad move northward from the Chesapeake Bay. In years in which there is a late winter run-off, there tends to be a reduced haul because the shad swim under the nets in the high waters. (Photograph courtesy of Yvonne Warren.)

We will all be forever grateful to photographers such as Frank Fritz. In this image he has captured the tranquility of these two men sitting by the Delaware and looking over to New Hope. Fritz operated his studios at 32 and also 46 1/2 North Union Street in Lambertville from the 1860s through the gay '90s. (Photograph courtesy of Joseph Cavallaro.)

Miss Hannah Anderson was the daughter of J.A. Anderson. She was escorted by her beau to Washington's Rock on Goat Hill for this photograph, taken by her father. (Photograph courtesy of George Kline.)

The Kalmia Club's clubhouse is located next to Sheridan Park in Lambertville. This structure was originally built as a Friends Meeting House. In 1910, it was given to the Kalmia, a women's literary and cultural club that was organized in 1892 and is still active today. (Photograph courtesy of Yvonne Warren.)

Many fraternal, social, and cultural organizations had meeting halls with facilities for playing pool, dominoes, and cards, as well as for discussing politics over a fine cigar. Here we see the members of the Mystic Chain. The secret Order of Druids was located in nearby Flemington. (Photograph courtesy of Lambertville Historical Society.)

The Chautauqua traveling culture show set up along North Main Street in New Hope in 1915. It offered stories and games for children, as well as dance, theater, music, and lectures. It provided much more than the mere sensation offered to the MTV generation. The Reverend Russell Conwell gave his "Acres of Diamonds" lecture and used the money raised helped to found Temple University. The Chautauqua was not the only traveling show to visit the community. The Kleckner & Company Monster Circus, Museum, Caravan & Menagerie also came to town on occasion. (Photograph courtesy of James Magill.)

The unforgettable Miss Pearl White was brought to town in 1914 for the filming of an episode of the *Perils of Pauline*. Miss White stayed at the Lambertville House and shot a scene at New Hope's most dangerous curve in the railway. Iris H. Naylor's column in *The Beacon*, "Footprints in the Valley," offers weekly remembrances of similar events in days gone by. (Photograph courtesy of James Mastrich and Kathryn Hall.)

Old-timers fondly remember having many pageants and festivals. Many of the revelers in this photograph may have come from the Holmquist School, which was a girls school in New Hope located on the grounds of the current La Bonne Auberge. In addition to the visits by traveling circuit performers such as Chautauqua, there were also local centers for the performing arts. The Music Circus on Music Mountain and the Bucks County Playhouse on the Delaware River offered a variety of Broadway and off-Broadway performances and concerts for the pleasure of the community. Local actors would support famous thespians in these productions. Visitors came from far and wide to get some "culture" and continue to do so to this day. (Photograph courtesy of James Magill.)

Edward Redfield, a renowned member of the New Hope School of Painting, rendered this painting of the Parry Mansion. The historic Parry Mansion is located in the center of New Hope across from the Logan Inn and near the Bucks County Playhouse. (Photograph courtesy of James Magill.)

Three women and a man: let your imagination take you where it will! (Photograph courtesy of Lambertville Historical Society.)

The Stockton Inn was built in 1710 as a private residence. By 1888, it was known as the Hockenbury Hotel. In 1936, the Rodgers and Hart song "There's a Small Hotel with a Wishing Well" was performed in the Broadway hit *On Your Toes*. The song was inspired by the Stockton Inn (the small hotel) and the lovely steeple of the Presbyterian church down the lane. The inn continues to be known for its fine food and lodging.

Sharp's Studio in Trenton captured the charm of the little representative of Lambertville on the left. The photograph on the right, of Emma McNeal, was taken at Tibbel's Art Studio in Lambertville. An advertisement for Hennigar's Photograph Gallery, a competitor of Tibbel's, reads: "If you want your picture good and cheap, Come to my place in Church on Union Street. For pictures in locket, ring or letter, In Lambertville you'll not find better . . If a person is sick or deceased at your home, To get their picture to me you must come, With their EYES OPEN, as natural as life, And your babies, bless their hearts! tell your wife, I've got patience, I'm sure to get them, For I've got a peculiar way to sett them, Pictures copied, large or small, Satisfaction guaranteed to all." (Photograph courtesy of Lambertville Historical Society.)

This lovely view of Lambertville and New Hope was taken from Goat Hill, also known locally as Washington's Table. The great general and national patriarch enjoyed this view many years before. (Photograph courtesy of George Kline.)